T0304408

The Little Encyclopedia of

ENCHANTED WOODLAND CREATURES

The Little Encyclopedia of

ENCHANTED WOODLAND CREATURES

An **A-to-Z Guide** to

Mythical Beings of the Forest

Jason Lancaster

Illustrated by Kate Forrester

RUNNING PRESS
PHILADELPHIA

Text copyright © 2024 by Running Press
Interior and cover illustrations copyright © 2024 by Kate Forrester
Cover copyright © 2024 by Hachette Book Group, Inc.

Running Press
Hachette Book Group
1290 Avenue of the Americas, New York, NY 10104
www.runningpress.com
@Running_Press

First Edition: October 2024

Published by Running Press, an imprint of Hachette Book Group, Inc. The Running Press name and logo are trademarks of Hachette Book Group, Inc.

The Hachette Speakers Bureau provides a wide range of authors for speaking events. To find out more, go to www.hachettespeakersbureau.com or email HachetteSpeakers@hbgusa.com.

Running Press books may be purchased in bulk for business, educational, or promotional use. For more information, please contact your local bookseller or the Hachette Book Group Special Markets Department at Special.Markets@hbgusa.com.

Print book cover and interior design by Katie Benezra
Written by Jason Lancaster

Library of Congress Cataloging-in-Publication Data
Names: Lancaster, Jason, author. | Forrester, Kate, illustrator.
Title: The little encyclopedia of enchanted woodland creatures : an A-to-Z guide to mythical beings of the forest / Jason Lancaster ; illustrated by Kate Forrester.
Description: First edition. | Philadelphia : Running Press, [2024] | Includes bibliographical references and index.
Identifiers: LCCN 2024015313 (print) | LCCN 2024015314 (ebook) | ISBN 9780762486137 (hardcover) | ISBN 9780762488360 (ebook)
Subjects: LCSH: Forests and forestry—Folklore. | Animals, Mythical. | Forest animals—Habitat.
Classification: LCC GR785 .L36 2024 (print) | LCC GR785 (ebook) | DDC 398.24/540915203—dc23/eng/20240606
LC record available at https://lccn.loc.gov/2024015313
LC ebook record available at https://lccn.loc.gov/2024015314

ISBNs: 978-0-7624-8613-7 (hardcover), 978-0-7624-8836-0 (ebook)

Printed in the United States of America

LSC-C

Printing 1, 2024

CONTENTS

INTRODUCTION

Throughout history, forests have been known to be full of danger, fascination, and mystery. To walk into a forest is to open up to the possibility of unexpected adventure. The forest is a place for dreamers, explorers, and those in need of escape. Fairy tales and folklore are often set in enchanted forests. Some ancient tales of the woodlands were told to try to explain the unexplainable. Some have religious origins. Cultural legends and shared stories have planted seeds of woodland enchantment in all of us. People young and old enter a woodland longing to find a flicker of magic—something fascinating that could change their lives forever. The enchanted forest is a hiding place, a place of rest. A delightful realm where trees can talk, and damsels are hidden for knights to rescue. Enchanted woodland stories often feature humanlike creatures, whether they be tiny pixies or towering giants. Some of them have origin stories that go back from before the Earth was formed. Other stories feature creatures that have been created out of human strife, the Earth itself, or simply for entertainment.

Almost all enchanted creatures are said to keep their distance from humans, but there are some who can speak a traveler's language, some who are looking to help or to hurt, to trick or to heal, or to capture and, possibly, to kill. In the days of yore, many tales of the forest and its alluring enchantments were used by well-meaning elders to scare children from going too far into the woods. Others were told by those who claimed to have set eyes on, communicated with, fought, or run away from otherworldly creatures, magical animals, or spirits themselves.

Enchanted woodland creatures have been part of the thread of cultures throughout the world. They are the mascots for sports teams, they are depicted on the columns of ancient temples, they're in children's books, on T-shirts, in the folklores and stories we will continue to tell and be fascinated by.

So, who are some of these creatures and where do they come from? Are any of them real? If we walked into the forest at the right or wrong time under the right or wrong circumstances, may we in fact come upon fairies dancing in a clearing? Or perhaps a hellhound? The Jersey Devil. Or maybe Athena's owl beckoning us on toward a great adventure. Regardless, it's best to know what's out there, because as you'll see in this compilation, there are many mischievous enchanted creatures roaming the wild forest.

ENCHANTED
WOODLAND
CREATURES

A

AGROPELTER

THE AGROPELTER IS a fearsome critter deeply rooted in American folklore. According to legend, it is said to inhabit the dense forests of conifer trees, spanning from Maine to Oregon. The creature gets its name from the words *aggro*, meaning aggressive, and *pelt*, referring to the act of throwing objects. The Agropelter dwells within hollow trees, utilizing these natural hideouts as its vantage point and patiently awaiting unsuspecting passersby or intruders who venture too close to its domain. In an act of aggression or self-defense, the creature hurls wooden splinters and branches at its targets with remarkable precision. According to some accounts, the creature is so swift that it has never been directly observed by humans. Instead, it remains an elusive and mysterious entity, striking from the shadows and disappearing into the depths of the forest before anyone can catch a glimpse of it.

AL-MI'RAJ

WITH ITS BLACK horn and yellow-golden fur, this horned hare is originally found in the tales of Arabic legend and is said to originate from a dragon-laden island off the coast of West Africa. Al-Mi'raj, unlike its Leporidae kin, the jackalope, has only one horn, resembling a unicorn horn rather than antlers. This tremendous creature is known for its ability to drive away an animal who looks at it with just one glance. There are ancient tales of Alexander the Great owning this horned hare as a pet. Hailing from a forest island in which dragons roamed, there are also legends of the Al-Mi'raj slaying dragons by feeding them poisoned meat.

ANANSI

THE STORY OF Anansi the spider originated in West African folklore and was passed through the Caribbean and then to America through the trafficking of enslaved people. Although most traditional stories depict him as a trickster, Anansi is seen as a sort of flawed genius, as most of his trickster ways are used as a means to attain wisdom and freedom. But sometimes he makes big mistakes with serious consequences. One such story recounts Anansi hiding all the wisdom in the world in a pot in the forest, only for the rain to wash away the pot of wisdom forever. There are chronicles of his fight against Death. Stories of Anansi were also used by enslaved people to instruct, entertain, and speak in code about their desire for freedom and the dangerous decisions they were forced to make to stay alive. Anansi is an important and powerful spider of the forest.

ANDVARI

A DWARF FROM Norse mythology, Andvari
lives under a waterfall, guarding his precious
treasures: a hoard of gold as well as a magical
ring called the Andvaranaut, which is said to
bring immense fortune to its possessor. He
is a solitary creature who only cares about
protecting his fortune. Beware, for he is also
known for his curse, which brings misfor-
tune and tragedy to anyone who would dare

steal his riches. He has the power to turn into a pike, seeking refuge in the depths of the river to protect himself if necessary.

AZEBAN

IN ABENAKI AND Penobscot legend, Azeban is the name of a trickster raccoon, whose exploits were highlighted in many stories meant for children. In these stories, the creature gets into mischief that impacts others, but unlike many other tales told of more nefarious creatures, Azeban is not dangerous. The stories shared are often humorous, and they reflect many common perceptions of the creatures. The same cleverness and curiosity in raccoons can both inspire and distress humans, depending on the time and place of their escapades. Raccoons have a tendency to behave unexpectedly, and this has made the mischievous animal an impeccable archetype for a lighthearted lesson.

B

BABA YAGA

STORIES OF BABA Yaga are deeply rooted in Slavic folklore. She is an old, haggard witch with iron teeth and a long, crooked nose. Deep within the forest, she lives in a remote hut that is situated atop chicken legs that she can manipulate and rotate. This peculiar abode is surrounded by a fence made of human bones and topped with skulls, serving as a chilling warning to all who approach. She possesses strong magical powers and is known to be a guardian of the forest and its creatures as well as a wise and cunning sorceress. While she can be unpredictable and even evil, she's also known to be a valuable acquaintance, offering guidance to those who prove themselves worthy. Her wisdom is sought by those brave or desperate enough to seek her out, but her aid is never given freely. Baba Yaga presents her visitors with impossible tasks or riddles to solve, testing their worthiness and resourcefulness.

BAKU

THE BAKU ARE forest creatures that come from Japanese folklore. They are ethereal beings that live deep within dense forests, and they are described as a mashup of animals, made up of the body of a bear, the head of an elephant, the eyes of a

rhinoceros, the tail of an ox, and the legs
of a tiger. Yet, despite that frightening
description, the baku are known as being
forces for good—and protectors of humankind. They are celebrated for their ability
to devour nightmares and bring peace to
those haunted by terrible dreams. Being in
a baku's presence promises health and good
fortune. In ancient Japanese culture, some
embroidered pillows were made with the
kanji styling of "baku" to ward off nightmares, illness, and evil spirits. Some people
consider baku to be holy. In some places,
there are drawings of baku etched into the
doorways and columns of temples.

BALL-TAILED CAT

THE BALL-TAILED CAT, also known as *Felis caudaglobosa*, is a fearsome creature from North American folklore, often described as resembling a mountain lion but with one striking difference—an unusually long tail ending in a solid, bulbous mass. According to foresters' tales from the turn of the twentieth century, this distinctive appendage served as a powerful weapon for striking down its prey. As the stories go, encounters with ball-tailed cats were common among homesteaders, who shared various versions of the creature's characteristics and abilities. One of the more prominent variants is the "digmaul," a ball-tailed cat known for its extraordinary tail, which is said to pack a powerful punch, delivering deadly blows to its victims. Another variation is the "sliver cat," which not only possesses a smooth-sided ball for knocking wayfarers unconscious but also boasts a spiked side that is capable of piercing and grappling its unfortunate targets.

BASILISK

APPEARING IN EUROPEAN folklore, bestiaries, and famous written works, the basilisk is a legendary creature often depicted as a serpent with the ability to petrify or kill with just one look. Known by some as the king of the snakes, the basilisk is said to possess deadly and potent venom capable of poisoning the land it traverses, leaving a trail of dead vegetation in its wake. Legends

describe the basilisk as a hybrid creature with features of a serpent and a rooster, often portrayed with a crown or crest on its head. Stories surrounding the basilisk have evolved over time, but they generally agree that encounters with this creature are dangerous and should be avoided. It is said to dwell in dark and desolate places, such as deep forest caves or abandoned ruins. In some tales, this creature is described as a serpent with wings, capable of flight.

BELLED BUZZARD

HAILING FROM THE treetops of North Carolina or Tennessee, this singular bird of prey has been said to not just be a carrion bird, feeding on the flesh of dead animals, but as both an omen of death and a portent of new life. There have been accounts in the United States of the solo Belled Buzzard traveling throughout the South since the mid-1840s. It is spotted typically only when in flight—when the sound of its bell catches the ear of unsuspecting humans on the ground below. As one might expect, its spooky familiarity to the turkey vulture indeed associates this creature with death. Its echoic bell's ring is seen as an undertaker's call. But to many still, the jingling of the Belled Buzzard can also be interpreted as an announcement of a baby yet to come to the family who hears it. The Belled Buzzard has even been known to replace the more commonly cited stork in regional lore about the arrival of a new baby.

BIGFOOT

ALSO KNOWN AS Sasquatch, Bigfoot is
a legendary creature that has become an
iconic figure in cryptozoology and folklore.
Described as an elusive humanoid creature,
Bigfoot is believed to inhabit remote forests
and wilderness areas, primarily in North
America. Bigfoot is often depicted as tall
and covered in shaggy hair, with enormous
footprints suggesting its massive size.
Sightings and reports of the creature have
fueled speculation about its existence, while
blurry photographs, inconclusive evidence,
and compelling eyewitness testimonies continue to contribute to its enduring mystery.

BR'ER RABBIT

BR'ER RABBIT IS a clever and mischievous character from African American folklore known for his escapades in the enchanting woods. With the forest as his playground, Br'er Rabbit's cunning tricks and cleverness shine through as he outsmarts his fellow woodland creatures like Br'er Fox and Br'er Bear. The woods serve as a backdrop for Br'er Rabbit's adventures, where he darts between trees, hides in thickets, and finds refuge in the embrace of nature. Within the woods, Br'er Rabbit's resourcefulness and ability to think on his feet are his greatest strengths. There's fun to be had in his mischief—just try not to be the recipient.

C

CAMAZOTZ

FROM ANCIENT MAYAN mythology, Camazotz is a giant vampire bat—also known as the Death Bat—who works for the lords of the underworld. Like all bats, this bat is nocturnal. He feeds on blood, and there are stories of Camazotz searching for and killing unsheltered humans in the dark forest. There are also stories of Camazotz giving humans the knowledge of fire. Some Mayan beliefs elevate the Camazotz to the stature of a god—the god of death, darkness, and sacrifice.

CHICKCHARNEY

THIS ENCHANTED FLIGHTLESS owl can be found on Andros Island in the Bahamas, nested among several pine trees bound together. Standing one meter tall, with a large owl-like body and extra-long legs, this red-eyed bird being is known to bring either good or bad luck to travelers who come across its path, depending on how they treat the creature. When met with kind treatment, the chickcharney is said to bestow luck upon its visitors, but should one disrespect, mock, or insult it, then pain and despair shall await them. Children are told to beware of the chickcharney—that it can snatch young people who may be traveling alone or even when they're lying asleep in their beds. The stories of these birds are used as a cautionary tale, and most people in the region are advised to keep bright cloth on them at all times; sharp colors charm and pacify the creature.

D

DRAGONS

A WORLDWIDE MYTHICAL phenomenon, dragons have been described in many different ways. In some cultures, they are wingless and snakelike, but the common image of the modern dragon is a large reptilian winged creature with the ability to breathe fire. Some say that the stories of dragons

might have come from ancient discoveries of
dinosaur bones. Forest dragons are said to be
green, which is great for blending in—something these creatures need. They like to hang
out deep in the forest, living in caves or near
swamps. Dragons are known to sometimes
interact with humans. They are reported to
love treasure and food, both of which they
would guard with their lives. Demanding sacrifices, dragons have threatened some people,
and they will eat entire flocks of sheep and
see whole villages burned. But there are also
tales of friendly dragons that will die for the
people and dragons they love. There, too,
are stories of dragons that can't blow fire
at all. And there are many figures who have
perished in classic tales and folklore while
trying to discern which kind of dragon they
were dealing with.

DRYAD

IN GREEK MYTHOLOGY, there is an other-worldly presence that breathes life into the heart of the forest. These enchanted woodland creatures are known as dryads, tree nymphs, or tree spirits, and they share a bond with all living flora.

The word *dryad* is derived from the Greek word *drys*, which means "oak." At first, the word only applied to nymphs connected to oak trees, but over time this definition expanded to encompass all tree nymphs. Dryads are known for their heavenly beauty and also their shyness. The only non-nymph they are said to regularly interact with is the goddess Artemis, known for her deep connection to nature. Around their friend Artemis, dryads are eager to speak their minds.

The gods entrusted dryads with safeguarding all forests and blessing all groves. The hamadryads are a subspecies that are known to merge with their tree's very essence, which means their fate mirrors that of the tree. When the tree dies, they die, or vice versa. The dryads' sacred connection with trees helps explain the respect that Greek gods and mortals paid to the woodlands.

In John Milton's *Paradise Lost*, they evoke elegance. John Keats's "Ode to a Nightingale" describes them as "light-winged Dryad[s] of the trees." Poets like Sylvia Plath used them as symbols to evoke the essence of nature.

Dryads epitomize the harmonious interplay between humanity and the natural realm, from the secrets whispered by ancient oaks to the gentle rustling of leaves in the breeze. Tree nymphs beckon the curious and imaginative to explore a realm where myth and reality intertwine. In this enchanted realm, every tree harbors a guardian spirit.

Notable Dryads in Greek Mythology:

1. The Meliae: Nymphs of the ash tree and nurturers of Zeus.
2. The Oreads: Nymphs linked with mountain conifers.
3. Hamadryads: Permanently connected to oak and poplar trees. They are guardians of river trees and groves.
4. The Maliades: Associated with fruit trees and known as protectors of sheep.
5. The Daphnaie: Known for a divine presence. Found in laurel trees.

E

ENCHANTED FOREST

WHEREVER THERE ARE forests, there are stories, folklore, myths, and spiritual practices that are tied to the woods and the creatures that live there. Tales told about the woodlands invoke the enchantment of these ever-changing environments, thick with flora and fauna and teeming with mystery and possibility. It is through the appeal of this possibility that the unfamiliar and the unknown draw their power. The joy and wonder that may lay beyond the entrance of the woods is balanced with its potential for danger. So, the stories of the woodlands

reflect many of the greatest tales of human history, where often great risk results in great reward or great harm, depending on the tools, skills, knowledge, luck, intentions, and temperaments of those who cross the threshold of the forest. A seducing sense of beauty is found in the deep forest. A rustling in the bushes can cause spine-tingling fear, or it can reveal the wind flowing over unknown rivers, lakes, streams, valleys, clearings, or the enchanted creatures that live there. The forest is budding with magical tales partly because most humans don't dwell in them. Trees are cut down to make way for society, forging human shelter and convenience out of nature and its magic—from the most awe-inspiring old trees and abundant flowers to fruit that can either satiate or

kill and adorable animals that cuddle
or attack.

ENTS

ENTS ARE ANCIENT creatures from the
writer J. R. R. Tolkien's Middle-earth in
The Lord of the Rings. They are guardians
of the trees. These beings, reminiscent of
trees themselves, harbor a connection to
Dwarves in their origin. Yavanna's plea to
Eru, inspired by Aulë's creation of Dwarves,
led to the birth of Ents. Ents are thought
to have been either souls inhabiting trees
or beings that evolved to resemble trees due
to their deep love for them. Ents emerged
as protectors of the forests at the behest
of Yavanna, a powerful being who, like

the Ents, is said to have existed since the beginning of time. They guard against threats like Orcs and Dwarves.

F

FAUNS

ACCORDING TO ANCIENT Greek mythology, the faun is half man, half goat. Renaissance-era depictions added pointed ears. Although they have been known to strike fear in the hearts of lost forest travelers, they are mostly peaceful and fun-loving creatures that are willing to serve as guides to those who need their help. The ancient Greek god Pan, who

was god of the wild, flocks, and shepherds, was depicted as a faun-like creature, and there are stories of Pan using the fauns as his official guides. Fauns can be found in many classic works of art, literature, and music. In a forest, which can feel increasingly frightening the more lost one becomes, it is never a bad sight to meet a friendly faun willing to help guide you home.

G

GHOSTS

THE FOREST IS full of enchanted ghosts and spirits, some of whom you will find in this little encyclopedia. The enchanted forest has long been thought of as a place for souls after their deaths, especially humans who died in battle or under mysterious circumstances. Some of these ghosts are harmless, while others are hell-bent on finding justice, redemption, or peace long after their deaths.

GLAWACKUS

A LEGEND FROM the stories of nineteenth- and twentieth-century North American lumberjacks, the glawackus is also known as the Northern Devil Cat. It has been described as looking like a mix between a

lion, a bear, and a panther. This fearsome critter is blind and uses its super senses of both hearing and smell to get around. It screeches like a hyena. Farm animals and pets have been known to go missing or die with the glawackus emerging as the most likely suspect, especially in Glastonbury, Connecticut, where the Northern Devil Cat was once spotted by hundreds of people in 1939. All forest searches and hunts for the glawackus have come up with nothing. But even if you were to spot one in the wild, you might not remember. One look into its devilish eyes will erase your memory of ever having seen it.

GNOMES

A FAMILIAR CREATURE made famous by
its depiction as a lawn ornament in many
a garden, the gnome is a mythical being
steeped in folklore and legend. These small,
humanlike creatures first came to light in
Western European folklore, particularly
from Germany. Gnomes were originally
believed to live mostly in the woods and
underground, guarding precious treasures
hidden deep within the earth. Gnomes
became even more famous in the nineteenth
century in stories by the Brothers Grimm
and Hans Christian Andersen. In these
tales, they are portrayed as tiny, bearded
creatures wearing pointed hats and living in
woodland burrows or hollow trees. Gnomes
are known to be protectors of the natural

world. They are guardians of nature who nurture both plants and animals. They are associated with good luck and fortune. Gnomes are considered wise and knowledgeable beings, possessing an intimate understanding of the earth and its secrets. They can bring prosperity to those who treat them kindly.

GOBLINS

IN EUROPEAN FOLKLORE, a goblin is a small grotesque creature similar in stature to a dwarf. Like many creatures of the forest, there are numerous tales of goblins as tricksters that possess the magical ability to shape-shift. There are also stories, however, where goblins are known as friendly and

fun creatures. The original English transla-
tion of *The Smurfs* describes the creatures as
"goblins." And like those beloved Belgian
comics, there is a long history of folklore
that features stories of goblins living in the
woods or forest caves, but unlike the lovable
blue Smurfs, most goblins are described
as being ugly enough to frighten anyone
who stumbles across them. In many stories,
goblins are tiny monsters with big plans,

like abducting a princess and forcing her to marry their goblin prince or stealing a pony. In many modern stories, goblins have been depicted as everything from completely evil and living in caves to kind-hearted railway workers known to possess an aptitude for mechanics and machinery.

HELLHOUND

A FIGURE FOUND in mythologies from all around the world, the hellhound is usually depicted as a giant black dog that is supernaturally strong and often moving in a trail of flames. In many mythologies, hellhounds are believed to guard the gates of the underworld. And in case you were wondering, where else would the gates to hell be but deep inside the forest? Some cultures believe that hellhounds eat corpses, and other cultures believe hellhounds can shoot fire out of their mouths. Some say a single hellhound could be the devil in disguise. Nineteenth-century Connecticut folklore says the Black Dog is death itself. Hellhounds are depicted in many video games and board games, sometimes appearing differently than they did in old folklore but never appearing as a creature you'd like to get mixed up with. Hellhounds are to be avoided.

HUGAG

YET ANOTHER FEARSOME critter of North American lore, the hugag is a beast of unfathomable size in the Northwoods. Despite its foreboding stature, it is unfortunately unable to sit down. Its only respite comes in the form of leaning up against trees in the forests of Minnesota, Wisconsin, and Canada, where it is known to dwell. The hugag's legs resemble tree trunks, rough and unbending. Its furry green coat is the texture of pine needles. With a moose-like body and a face that hangs down into a bill of sorts, this unusual creature would be a sight to see among lumberjacks of yore. Hugags are generally known to be peaceful herbivores, going to great lengths to avoid interacting with humans.

HULDRA/HULDER

HAILING FROM THE folklore of both
Germany and Norway, the huldra/hulder
has been described as a feminine figure,
lithe and blond, but with a foxtail or a
cow's tail—and a back that resembles the
bark of a hollowed-out tree trunk. This
perplexing maiden is known to be cunning
and seductive, luring those who encounter
her deep into the forest and toward their
possible demise. Legend has it that some of
their victims are allowed to leave, should
they agree to marry the huldra, but following the union, the huldra's strength and
power increase, and the new spouse is likely
to fall victim to it all the same. However,
there are also tales of neutral interactions
with huldra, and even a few stories wherein

the huldra have been kind and bestowed luck upon children who have crossed their path. Huldra are said to embody the beauty and danger of the forest; their name comes from a Scandinavian word for "covered" or "hidden." The legends of huldra serve as a cautionary tale for those who feel pulled toward the beauty of the unknown. Little is known about her masculine counterpart, the huldrekall, other than that he is a hideous creature, dwelling underground in the forest.

HULI JING

UNLIKE THE *KITSUNE* (see page 51), most Huli Jing are said to have nine tails. They are misunderstood, with the weight of their legend leaning more toward evil than not, but many of the stories told about them reveal their kindness and generosity. These opposing perspectives make the Huli Jing hard to pin down, which suits them well, as Huli Jing are known to be shape-shifters, changing form and voice and increasing in power over time. The powerful magic of the Huli Jing may leave many people quaking in fear since stealing a person's essence is said to be what the Huli Jing seek on the path of their own spiritual journeys. According to legend, they gain power through stealing a sleeping human's breath, or embodying human form and manipulating another human into a sexual interaction. Only through these extractive exploitations are they able to gain the vitality they so desire.

J

JACKALOPE

KNOWN AS THE hybrid of a jackrabbit and an antelope, or in some accounts, a mashup of a jackrabbit and a mule deer, the jackalope has the hopping proclivity of a hare, the antlers of an antelope, and the speed of both animals. This creature of North American legend is said to have tormented loggers and homesteaders throughout history by attacking with their antlers. It is also known as a master of deception and distraction, as it can imitate the sound of all kinds of animals, including, most notably, human voices. Due

to its own pernicious nature, the jackalope
is ever on watch, even going so far as to
walk backward into its burrow in order to
be on the defense against any creature that
dare try to be its predator. It is rumored
to be quelled only by a drink of whiskey,
as was discovered by humans in a quest for
the jackalope's prized mammalian milk.
Adding to its peculiarity, the jackalope
is said to only procreate during lightning
storms, the relative infrequency of which
surely contributes to their rarity in the wild.

JERSEY DEVIL

SAID TO INHABIT the Pine Barrens forests of
southern New Jersey in the United States,
tales of this enchanted woodland creature

have been part of the region's folklore and
culture since the seventeenth century. With
hundreds of reported sightings throughout
the years, descriptions of the creature vary.
One thing most seem to agree on is that the
Jersey Devil is fast, has horns and a terrify-
ing high-pitched scream, and can fly with
its bat-like wings. More practical story-
tellers believe the Jersey Devil is actually
a sandhill crane that has been mistaken

for an otherworldly creature. It has been accused of killing scores of livestock. In more modern times, it has been depicted as a more traditional devil. The New Jersey Devils hockey team is named after the Jersey Devil, and their logo prominently features the creature's horns and tail. Even though it has become more commercialized and depicted in movies and comic books, there are still those who believe the Jersey Devil roams the forests of the Pine Barrens and continue to hunt for it to prove that it is real.

K

KELPIES

A KELPIE IS a shape-shifting sprite that often takes the form of a horse and is also able to appear as a human. They have a beautiful black mane and an impressive stature, but their looks can be deceiving. Part of Scottish folklore, kelpies are believed to inhabit every Scottish river, stream, and lake. Their method of destruction is to trick people, often children, into hopping on their backs for a gallop along the water, only to then jump into the river and drown their unsuspecting riders. In some cases, a kelpie will take its victims underwater, eat them, and leave only their entrails behind. They are mostly solitary creatures, and some say that what makes them different from normal horses—besides their penchant for eating people!—is their inverted hooves.

KITSUNE

THESE LONG-LIVED FOX spirits of Japanese lore possess magical gifts. Said to enjoy fried tofu, these divine messengers are fox-like creatures that have gained power and abilities over the course of many decades, or in some cases, hundreds of years. They have many descriptors, as there are thirteen kinds of kitsune in Japanese mythology, and each type is represented by a component of the natural world (Darkness, Wind, Fire,

Earth, Forest, River, Ocean, and Mountain),
or the divine (Heaven and Spirit). The kitsune are also all positioned on the spectrum
between good and evil. The most fearsome
kitsune are known to trick humans,
luring unsuspecting people into
traps, or possessing and tor-
turing their souls. But
on the other hand,
many kitsune
are known
to emanate
kindness and
abundance,
including
granting
bountiful
crop yields
and financial

prosperity to those who offer them gifts and reverence. The most powerful kitsune, the Tenko (Heaven) kitsune, is said to have lived for one thousand years and to possess nine tails, whereas most kitsune have fewer. Along its journey to prominence, the Tenko kitsune have gained powers beyond embodying human form, including manipulating space and time and becoming all-knowing and celestial. The kitsune have similarities to, but also stark differences from, the Huli Jing of Chinese folklore and the Kumiho of Korean legend.

KUMIHO

THE HULI JING invoke fear in many, but even more malicious are the Kumiho. The

Kumiho are the evilest of these legendary foxes. Like the other fox spirits, the Kumiho is known to transform into human form and seduce humans in order to steal their essences or else to harm the human spirit. However, the Kumiho is the only fox spirit known to kill people and consume their flesh. Korean folklore reveals that Kumiho experience a burning desire to take on human form, and through a variety of challenges, they can surmount the evil in which they dwell in order to become a human permanently. These challenges include things such as refusing to kill or eat a human for one thousand days, or hiding their true form from humans for one hundred days, as well as doing other good deeds and generally not causing harm. If they do not succeed in their quest, they will lose the chance to become human and risk becoming a demon.

L

LEPRECHAUNS

THINKING OF A pot of gold on the forest floor at the end of a rainbow? The only way to find the gold is by following a leprechaun to his treasure. If you catch a leprechaun, they will grant you three wishes. But watch out because they are also known to be tricksters as well as good company, a dangerous combination. Leprechauns come from Irish folklore. For a long time they

were believed to be real,
and to this day they are
universally known
as a symbol
of good luck.
These fairylike
creatures are short
in stature, and they
wear big green
hats with black
straps, gold
buckles galore,
long beards, green
jackets, and big
shoes. You can
see them smiling
on cereal boxes,
used as mascots for
various sports teams,

and plastered all over towns as decorations around St. Patrick's Day. But to find one in the forest, maybe even a group of them dancing to a traditional Irish song, repairing shoes with tiny hammers, or fiercely protecting their gold, would be a rare thing indeed. Whether you follow a leprechaun for their treasure, the three wishes they might grant you, or just out of pure curiosity, make sure you proceed with caution. And good luck!

LESHY

IN SLAVIC MYTHOLOGY, the leshy, whose Russian name translates to "[he/she] from the forest," is known as the guardian of woodlands and the ruler of hunting domains. The deity Svyatibor, known to eastern and western Slavs, is identified as the god of the forests and the lord of the leshies. Like many forest creatures, the leshy is also known to be a bit of a trickster. He has shape-shifting abilities and usually appears as a masculine, humanoid figure. He can change his stature from as small as a seed to as tall as the tallest tree in the forest. Because of humans' fires, hunting, and chopping down of trees, the leshy can be very wary of people. This concern comes from their deep love of the forest and the natural world. They are willing to work with humans who treat them and the woodlands with respect, but they can also cause a lot of pain and suffering to those who would dare mistreat the forest and its inhabitants.

LOUP-GAROU

THE FRENCH-CANADIAN LOUP-GAROU is
known as a human who can shape-shift into
an animal, most commonly a wolf or dog,
but on occasion other creatures such as a
pig, an ox, or a cat. Originally conceived as
a punishment for not observing specific religious demands, the curse of the loup-garou
would be inflicted on a person for 101 days,
turning them into an animal at night that
would then roam the wilderness. In order
to break the curse, it is imperative that the
loup-garou not reveal its condition, or even
its knowledge of werewolves, or else it risks
taking on the affliction permanently.

Throughout its lore, the loup-garou
has been made a scapegoat for things that
mysteriously go missing, or for unexpected

or unexplainable harms that come people's way. This made the character of the
loup-garou, and other similar werewolf
creatures, an easier target for the fervor
surrounding the persecution of anyone
suspected of possessing wolflike qualities.

As werewolf mythology traveled
with French people to North America,
the North American loup-garou legends
incorporated aspects of indigenous stories
about human-wolf transformations wherein
the werewolf often acted out in search of
retribution for their affliction.

N

NORTHERN CARDINAL

WHILE A COMMONPLACE bird in many
parts of North America, northern cardinals
are also a welcome sight within American
folklore. With their sweet songs and striking image, cardinals have long been seen
as messengers from loved ones who have
passed on into death. If you find yourself
spending time among the wooded areas
in the Midwest or eastern United States,
southern sections of Canada, or in Mexico
and parts of Central America, cardinals
make their presence known. They are
especially prevalent in areas near cemeteries,

adding to the power of their legend. Said
to remain within a small radius of where
they were born, and to form couples for
many years, the cardinal is also a bird that
represents the power of relationships and
lifelong connection. Even in the bleakness
of winter, a cardinal's dependability is
evident, and they can be a welcome sight
against a blanket of snow, leafless trees, or a
barren landscape. Rather than serving as an

omen of death and destruction like many of their fellow woodland creatures, cardinals are a symbol of peace in the afterlife, steadfastness, and love.

O

OBERON

ALTHOUGH FIRST MENTIONED in a thirteenth-century French poem, Oberon, the King of the Fairies, was made most famous in Shakespeare's *A Midsummer Night's Dream*. The mysterious King of the Fairies reigns with Queen Titania, orchestrating a captivating dance of love, chaos, and

wonder. Holding court in the enchanted
woodland, Oberon's presence commands
both awe and fascination. He may wear a
crown, but that doesn't mean he's above
pettiness. He's known to dabble in the lives
of both fairies and humans, using mostly
harmless pranks and spells. His lovely
singing voice can
resonate through
the woodlands
like a spellbinding
melody, altering
destinies and trans-
forming reality
itself. Despite his
delightful nature
within the
depths of the
mystical forest,

Oberon is a powerful force. He is a master of the mystical arts. His magical touch can both mend and shatter hearts.

OWLS

ENCHANTED OWLS HAVE been a fascinating part of various cultures and mythologies throughout history. These secretive creatures are often associated with wisdom, mystery, and supernatural powers. They have been depicted as symbols of both good and evil, guardians of knowledge, and messengers between worlds. Here are a few of the most fascinating enchanted owls:

- **Athena's Owl:** In Greek mythology, the goddess Athena is closely associated with an owl as her sacred animal. Her owl symbolizes wisdom and intelligence, attributes associated with Athena herself. This owl, sometimes referred to as the "Athene noctua," is often depicted accompanying Athena, either perched on her shoulder or flying beside her.

- **Hootenflute:** The Hootenflute is a legendary owl found in Irish folklore. It is described as an elusive, mischievous creature with iridescent feathers that change color in the moonlight. The Hootenflute is known for its enchanting hooting melodies, which have the power to entrance those who hear them. It is said to lead wanderers astray but can

also serve as a guide to lost souls, leading them back to safety.

- **Lepidopteran Owl:** The lepidopteran owl is a mystical creature from Chinese mythology. This magnificent owl has large, vividly colored wings resembling those of a butterfly, which allow it to fly gracefully and silently through the night. It is believed to possess profound wisdom and is often regarded as a symbol of transformation.

- **Strix:** The Strix comes from ancient Roman folklore. It is depicted as a nocturnal creature with the ability to shape-shift into a human form. The

Strix is associated with dark magic, often portrayed as a malevolent sorceress who seeks to harm or drain the life force of unsuspecting victims. Its eerie hooting is believed to foretell impending doom or imminent danger.

- **Yatagarasu:** In Japanese mythology, the Yatagarasu is a three-legged crow that sometimes takes the form of an owl. It is believed to be a messenger of the gods, guiding and protecting humans on their journeys.

P

PAPA BOIS

HIS NAME CAN be translated to "father of the woods," and Papa Bois is just that, serving as the protector of forests in the Caribbean, most notably in St. Lucia and Trinidad and Tobago. Depictions of Papa Bois reveal him to resemble both goat and human: a biped with hoofed feet, animalic legs, large horns atop his head, a human torso, and to varying degrees, a hairy face. He is known to be kind to humans, though it is important that humans are kind to him, too. It is especially significant that anyone who sees Papa Bois does not stare at his hooves, as doing so is considered offensive. Papa Bois is powerful and could be dangerous if provoked. Though he is not motivated to harm, he is instead driven primarily by care for the flora and fauna under his guard. Committed to all the plants and animals of the forests, he has been known to use his power to transform into other creatures in order to frighten humans and drive them away. He can

move with great speed and stealth, and it is said that he always keeps a cow horn on his belt or around his neck, so that he may blow into it to alert the forest dwellers that humans or other dangers are close by.

PAUL BUNYAN AND BABE THE BLUE OX

AS LEGEND WOULD have it, Paul Bunyan was the fastest and most skilled lumberjack in American history. Paul, who was larger than life from birth, was said to have been brought to his family by multiple storks. As a boy, Paul found a young ox stuck in an unusually blue bank of snow that had fallen in a winter's storm. He brought the ox home and warmed it by the fire. The young ox recovered, though the blue hue remained on its coat. Paul decided to call the ox Babe, and like Paul, Babe grew to an enormous size. Together, they would change the landscape of North America. Paul and his trusty sidekick, Babe the blue ox, gathered a crew of other large lumberjacks and a chef, and together they traversed the woodlands of the United States and Canada, clearing trees. Paul, Babe, and his seven axmen are credited with creating Puget Sound, as well as the grasslands of the Dakotas, the Grand Canyon, and the Great Lakes. Debate over Paul Bunyan's origins extends from Maine to Michigan to Minnesota, but across much of the northern US and Canada, his legend echoes through the stories passed on to children, and many regard him as a part of American history. It is said that

Paul Bunyan and Babe still spend their
summers in Minnesota, but under the cover
of woodlands, where they're able to move in
relative secrecy.

PIXIES

THESE ENCHANTED WOODLAND creatures
of British and Celtic folklore are known
by various names such as pisky, pixy, pixi,
and more. They are often associated with
the high moorland areas of Devon and
Cornwall. These small humanlike creatures
are believed to live in caves, tombs, old
forts, and graveyards. Pixies are short in
stature and generally characterized as
kind, mischievous, and childlike. It is not
uncommon to come upon a group of pixies

having a delightful party. They are lovers of
the night and enjoy dancing and wrestling.
They are said to have a special bond with
horses and are known to style a horse's
hair in ringlets while riding them through
the forest. Although most tales of pixies
describe them as saving weary travelers
from harm and blessing humans who are
friendly to them, not all stories of pixies
are happy ones. There are legends of pixies
stealing children and treasure, and some

stories describe them as naked or shoddily dressed. These days, however, pixies are mostly depicted as tiny, childlike creatures with pointy ears, pointy hats, and green clothing. Regardless of the tale, however, pixies are not too keen to interact with humans if they can avoid it.

R

ROUGAROU

WHERE THE LOUP-GAROU of French legend is known to only transform into a wolf at night, the Cajun Rougarou lives perpetually in its transformed state, reflected in depictions that feature a creature with a wolf's head and a human body. Making no efforts to evade humans, the Rougarou is far more ominous. Known for being highly intelligent and very difficult to best, the Rougarou has haunted the wooded bayous of Louisiana for centuries, and it is said to be lethal to Catholics who have not properly observed the practices of Lent. The legend of the Rougarou has long been used to scare children (and perhaps also adults) into compliance. Similarly to the loup-garou, Rougarous are said to be cursed for 101 days. However, rather than lifting the curse when their time is up, the affliction is simply given to another when the troubled Rougarou passes their burden on to a new victim by consuming the blood of an unaffected human.

RUSALKA

IN FORESTS, LAKES, rivers, and streams, these feminine mermaid-like creatures dwell. They are known to not take kindly to humankind, and many of them have the life experience to back up their distrust. Russian lore says the Rusalka are born from drowned women. Slavic lore tells us that a Rusalka is made from the soul of any young woman who has died near a river or lake

and has come back to haunt it. They are
tied to the water, like mermaids, but are
said to still have legs instead of fins. They
are very beautiful with long hair that is
always loose and are known to lure people
into the water to drown, sometimes being
submerged and tickled to death as the
Rusalka laughs.

Here are two fascinating Rusalka from
folklore:

Dana: Featured in a Russian folktale,
her wicked stepmother, envious of her
beauty, drowned Dana while they were
swimming near a water mill. Dana's
young groom longed for his late bride
and often visited the place of her death.
One night, he witnessed beautiful
maidens dancing on the wheels of the

mill, brushing their long green hair with white combs. Among them, he saw Dana and tried to reach her, but she vanished into the water. He dove after her but got entangled in her hair, leading him to an underwater palace. Dana warned him to leave immediately if he wanted to return to land, but the groom refused, declaring he could not live without her. Dana kissed him, and he transformed into the water king of that river.

Marina: A young widow from an old Simbirsk legend transformed into a Rusalka after drowning in the river. Legend claims she can take the form of a swan while swimming. She has been known to flip boats.

S

SASABONSAM

IN WEST AFRICAN folklore, the sasabonsam is a vampirish creature who lives in forest trees. It has been said to have long legs and feet with the ability to dangle its legs out of tree branches and snatch its victims from above. This vampire has been depicted as having bat-like wings and teeth made of iron. There is no indication in the mythology that these creatures are affected by the sun.

SPIRIT RABBIT
(JIIBAYAABOOZ)

THIS MYTHICAL HARE known as the Spirit
Rabbit is thought to have existed since
before the Earth began. In indigenous

Ojibwe folklore and stories from North America, he is known as a trickster who, on a deeper level, is dedicated to connecting the manitou (life force of all things) to the dreams of human beings. Even after his death, the "Ghost Rabbit," as he is also known, continued to teach and connect humans to the spirit world. Some tribes believe that Jiibayaabooz is responsible for humans' ability to have visions. Therefore, seeing his ghostly form in a forest is usually a sign that a deeper understanding of life and connection to all things is on the horizon.

SPLINTERCAT

PROWLING THE TOWERING forests of the Pacific Northwest, the Splintercat is said to

be the cause of one of the great mysteries
of the woodlands, the prevalence and
pattern of ragged, broken tree trunks. The
Splintercat is nocturnal, as cats are inclined
to be, and they prowl the night in search
of their favorite things to eat, namely:
raccoons, bees, and honey, all of which
are known to dwell in hollow trees. This
ferocious feline is said to bolt at incredible
speeds and launch into trees with its body,
shattering them and leaving behind ragged
dry splinters where their trunks once stood.
If a meal is revealed after such a pounce, the
Splintercat is delighted. If not, the destruc-
tive search continues.

SWAMP MONSTERS

ALL OVER THE world, wherever there are
forest swamps there are tales of monsters
living in their depths. Greek myth says the
monstrous Hydra was killed in a swamp by
Hercules. There is also the seven-foot-tall
Honey Island Swamp monster of Cajun
folklore that is said to live in a swamp in
Louisiana. There are tales of lizard men
in some swamps and skunk apes in others.
Some swamp monsters are said to be
humanlike and covered by the mud of the
swamp, while others are not thought to be
human at all, looking like moss or plants.
Either way, almost nothing good ever comes
from dealing with swamp monsters. The
will-o'-the-wisp on this list is another
example of one of these monsters. So,

wherever you are, if you see something
bubbling up out of the swamp, it's probably
best not to step any closer than necessary.

TĀNE

MĀORI (INDIGENOUS POLYNESIAN'S)
mythology says this god of forests and
birds is the son of the sky father and earth
mother. His parents held him and his
siblings in darkness until Tāne revolted
and split their parents apart. And thus, the
world as we know it began. Tāne's brother,
Tāwhirimātea, the god of storms, didn't

like that his brother had split their family apart, so he unleashed his wrath upon the earth and sea. Tāne's love was the forest, and Māori myth says his brother often tries to destroy it, killing all the trees and birds that he can. These battles over the earth and sea continue to this day. Tāne is said to have created the first man, Tiki, and from the soil of his mother earth, Tāne also created the first woman. He has provided humans with the things they need to fish and explore the sea, which is the realm of his brother, Tangaroa, who sometimes is seen in the form of a whale. This mythical lord of the forest watches over all humankind, especially citizens of the forest. Those who try to destroy the forest are his only enemies.

TEAKETTLER

AMID THE FORESTS of Minnesota and Wisconsin, there is said to dwell a doglike creature of short stature, with cat eyes and a curious habit of walking backward. Rarely seen but occasionally heard, this being of lumberjack lore gets its name from the steam that emerges from its snout and the high-pitched whistle it makes, not unlike, well, a teakettle.

TIKBALANG

THE TIKBALANG IS an enchanted creature from Philippine folklore. It is said to have superlong human limbs and the head of a horse. It lives in mountains and rainforests and is known to be a trickster that leads travelers astray, making the poor travelers go around in circles, and taking long journeys just to end up exactly where they started—lost. Some say a tikbalang is a ghost; others say it is a demon. There are many superstitions about how to deal with them, and some say if you walk quietly in the rainforest, the tikbalang won't notice you're there. Others say the trick is to wear one's shirt backward. It is said a sun-shower is a sign that a tikbalang is getting married.

TROLLS

SOMETIMES DEPICTED AS small, and other times large, according to the Nordic folklore or Norse mythology where they are mentioned, trolls dwell in isolated forest areas such as rocks, mountains, and caves, often living in small family units. In traditional tales, they don't enjoy interacting with humans, and some legends say they

could turn to stone if exposed to sunlight.
They do not like to travel far from their
homes. In some stories, trolls are known
to be very smart, very old, and very strong.
And while older tales may depict trolls as
smaller beings, more modern depictions,
like those in Tolkien's Middle-earth,
describe them as large, slow-moving, and
not very bright. Other stories recount trolls
as monsters known to kidnap humans.
Some modern tales also depict trolls as
adorable cartoonish creatures with pen-
chants for hugging, singing, and dancing.

ULUKAYIN

THE TREE OF life in Turkish mythology, Ulukayin, is commonly said to be either a beech or a poplar. This powerful tree serves as a bridge between the center of the Earth—that it reaches via its roots—and the sky, which it holds up with its branches. This tree is said to be a conduit of communication between the earth and sky, between life as we know it and life beyond. There are clear links between Ulukayin and the tree of life in Babylonian lore, an enchanted tree that grew in paradise, with roots dripping with the water of the first cells from which life emerged. Commonly depicted in religions throughout the world, as well as in popular culture, tree of life imagery has perhaps the furthest reach of any enchanted being of the woodland.

UNGNYEO

THE UNGNYEO IS the kind of forest creature that isn't so easy to identify at first. Known as the "bear woman" in Korean folklore, she is an important part of Korean creation myths and legends. It all started in a cave where a tiger and a bear became friends, both of them yearning to transcend their animal forms and become human. They asked the celestial king, Hwanung, to grant them their wishes. He told them they must

eat only twenty cloves of garlic and mug-
wort and to shun sunlight for one hundred
days. After twenty days, the tiger couldn't
take it anymore and left the cave for the
sun and a hunt; the bear, however, named
Ungnyeo, stayed in the cave and became a
woman on the twenty-first day.

Hwanung, moved by Ungnyeo's
loneliness when he spied her under a
sacred Betula tree and by her wish to be

a mother, eventually took her as his wife. Their union yielded a son named Dangun, who became the mythical founder of the Korean kingdom.

The narrative of Ungnyeo is layered with symbolism. She embodies the sacred lineage of the maternal deity, which is intricately woven into the Korean foundational narrative. This bears testament to the reverence accorded to both celestial and terrestrial forces, underscoring the profound unity between land and sky.

V

VODYANOY

WHAT'S THAT OVER there in the river? Is that a frog? No, its head is too big. The vodyanoy is often described as a naked old man donning a frog-like face, greenish beard, and tangled hair that's covered in algae and muck. Sporting webbed paws in place of hands, a fish's tail, and eyes that blaze like red-hot coals, the vodyanoy's body is adorned with black fish scales, earning him the endearing titles of "grand-father" and "forefather" from the locals. He rides the currents on a half-sunken log, creating resounding splashes as this strange

water spirit roams the waters. Believed
to be responsible for local drownings in
the Eastern European countries where his
story is told, he unleashes his might when
angered, breaking dams, destroying water
mills, and claiming the lives of people and
animals. To ward off his wrath, local fishers,
millers, and beekeepers offer him sacrifices.
Legend has it that a vodyanoy will sometimes drag a person down to his underwater
abode to make them his servant.

W

WAMPUS CAT

THE LEGEND OF the Wampus Cat paints this powerful beast as part cat and either part dog, amphibian, or human, depending on who regales you with the origin tale. And those who believe the Wampus Cat is part human again diverge on the particulars, though some commonalities are found. In various Appalachian tales, a woman was punished and transformed into the Wampus Cat after she was suspected of practicing witchcraft, while a story from the folklore of the Cherokee Nation features another woman who metamorphosed

into the Wampus Cat after she spied on a
sacred ritual by hiding under a mountain
lion's pelt. As a result, she forever lives
deep in densely wooded areas,
possessing a bone-chilling
scream that strikes fear
into the hearts of anyone
who hears it. Said to
have a prowess for
swimming, to be
fast and furtive
on land, to be
a consumer of
dogs, to chase
off humans with
a single glance of
her gleaming
green (or
sometimes

yellow) eyes, and to have either four or six legs, the legend of the Wampus Cat is larger than life. So much so that a number of high schools in the southern United States have chosen the Wampus Cat as their mascot.

WAQWAQ/WAKWAK TREE

WITH ROOTS IN Persian and Arabic lore, the singular Waqwaq Tree is said to grow on a wooded island in the East China Sea, where only women live. The Waqwaq Tree is the source of life in this community, wherein the population of the island grows from its branches. Some accounts have only humans growing from the tree, while other tales include mythical beings also sprouting from its branches. As the growing beings mature on the tree, they are said to shout "waq waq" upon dropping down to the ground, falling as a fruit would.

Similar legends are found in Chinese mythology, wherein a ginseng tree grows edible, fruit-shaped children, and the Japanese legend of Jinmenju, a tree whose blossoms are the heads of people.

WEREWOLVES

THE CATEGORY OF werewolf encompasses many mythologies about humans who could transform into wolves throughout antiquity. Many of these transformations have been said to occur in concert with a full moon, either of the human's own volition or after having been cursed. It is said that werewolf

mythology parallels that of witches, with their similarities in public perception, as well as persecution for intangible wrong-doing that others suspect. The rise of the "witch hunt" in Europe in the late Middle Ages resulted in a similar rise of the persecution of people accused of transforming into wolves, also known as lycanthropy.

WILL-O'-THE-WISP

THE WILL-O'-THE-WISP IS a mysterious and bewitching occurrence, and it has long intrigued folks across cultures and generations. These spectral lights flicker and dance in a blue or greenish hue above marshy areas and swamps, like ethereal lanterns casting a spell on weary forest travelers. The origin of these elusive lights remains a topic for debate, but they are thought to arise from the combustion of gases emitted by decaying organic matter. Throughout history, the will-o'-the-wisp has woven its way into myth and folklore, often attributed to fairies, spirits, or wandering souls, flickering and guiding wanderers into the unknown.

WITCHES OF THE FOREST

IN MANY FAIRY tales and myths, witches live and lurk in the woods. For most of history, societies have not looked kindly upon witches, so it makes sense that many of them would find themselves living in places where they can practice their craft somewhere mostly unbothered by humans. But not every witch in the forest wishes to avoid human contact. Some want unsuspecting humans to get lost and stumble into their lairs. Hansel and Gretel once found themselves lost amid the trees, stumbling upon an enchanting cottage made of gingerbread and sweets. Little did they know the cunning witch within would test their bravery and wit and turn the cottage into a trap. Much like the famed Baba Yaga of Slavic lore, witches are frequently depicted as guardians of the woodland's secrets, and their magic flows through its very roots. With gnarled staffs, they command nature, using herbs and alchemy to heal, protect, and cast spells.

Witches of the forest are keepers of the delicate balance between life and death.

They communicate with forest spirits and creatures and can bestow blessings upon those who approach them with respect. But those who seek to exploit their magic, or harm the forest, risk invoking their powerful hexes and curses. The trick to dealing with witches is keeping one's wits about and not assuming that every witch means to harm. A witch's magic can be used for good just as much as it can be used for evil.

WOLVES

THROUGHOUT THE WORLD there are tales of enchanted wolves roaming various forests. Both in history and folklore, wolves have been depicted as forces of good, evil, or a mix of both; they are bringers of light in some tales and harbingers of darkness in others. From grasslands to plains, wolves have often been seen as perplexing beings, linked with witchcraft, transformation, and rage. In German mythology, seeresses rode wolves, which highlights their connection to powerful and mystical forces. But in Navajo folklore, wolves are seen as witches in disguise. Tsilhqot'in tribes believed contact with wolves could bring about possible madness and death. Many Native American cultures also view wolves as bringers of medicine, success in hunting, and as embodiments of courage, strength, and loyalty. This is what makes wolves of the forest so captivating—they can be your friend, your protector, your guide, or they can be your greatest enemy and the last creature you will ever meet. Whether they appear as guardians of the forest in animated films like *Princess Mononoke* or as creatures embodying the spirit of independence in heavy metal music, wolves continue to captivate our imaginations as they roam the woodlands.

YGGDRASIL

THE YGGDRASIL'S NAME comes from an Old Norse term that means both "Odin's horse" and "gallows." This monumental ash tree is known as the "world tree" in Norse mythology. It holds an important role in

the cosmology of the Norse belief system. This awe-inspiring tree is the immense axis that interconnects nine realms, encompassing the celestial and the earthly, including the underworld, the world of humans, and the world of the gods. Yggdrasil embodies and is a symbol of both life and death. It serves as the gallows upon which Odin sacrifices himself to gain divine wisdom. Eagles and dragons live in this tree. It is

mentioned in ancient Norse texts such as
the *Poetic Edda* and the *Prose Edda* and plays a
vital role in the aftermath of Ragnarök, the
cataclysmic event symbolizing the end of
the world. You'll want to think twice before
trying to climb it.

CONCLUSION

I hope this encyclopedia of enchanted woodland creatures will spark your own imagination and sense of wonder. Inspire you to look out into the land with a magical lens, to find new and exciting adventures, to create your own stories of the forest and woodland creatures, because any rabbit you see hopping by can be as magical as you imagine, every tree able to move, every mouse capable of speaking. The strange bark you hear at night could be a dog, or it could be the mystical hoot of a magical owl sending an important message to those who know how to listen.

It is our human desire to explain what cannot be explained, and nature is where we live, we are part of it, and we humans love to tell and make up stories of its history, importance, and power. Most of the enchanted creatures in this list have never been seen or proven in a scientific way, but their stories have shaped nations and cultures throughout human history. And like the world we live in, stories of enchanted creatures continue to evolve, taking new shapes in movies, comic books, television, and literature.

The enchanted forest thrives on imagination, wonder, excitement, fear, and a desire for answers and for the world to be more than it often presents itself. Now, people may not believe in every single creature mentioned in this book or the countless others living in all the folklore, myths, and bedtime stories passed down through the ages, but most of us have at least one that we can't help but sort of believe in. The world is too beautiful, magical, mysterious,

and strange for there not to be at least one
of these enchanted woodland creatures out
there in the woods. For me, it's Bigfoot. I
can't say with 100 percent certainty that he
isn't real, but more than that, I believe he
must be part of a larger family, and maybe
in fact there is a whole species of Bigfoots.
And until someone can prove me wrong,
I will continue to search the Northwest
woods for larger-than-life footprints, and
if I come upon a witch or a talking frog, I
won't be all that surprised. May you enjoy
and stay safe on your forest adventures.

WORKS CITED

"Al-Mi'raj." *Wikipedia.* Last modified September 5,
    2023. https://en.wikipedia.org/wiki
    /Al-Mi%27raj.

"Al-Mihraj." *Fandom.* Accessed September 1, 2023.
    https://mythus.fandom.com/wiki/Al-Mihraj.

"al-Wakwak." *Wikipedia.* Last modified July 9,
    2023. https://en.wikipedia.org/wiki
    /Al-Wakwak.

"Are Kitsune and Huli Jing the Same?"
    StackExchange. Accessed September 1,
    2023. https://mythology
    .stackexchange.com/questions/213
    /are-kitsune-and-huli-jing-the-same.

"Baba Yaga." *Wikipedia.* Last modified November 8,
    2023. https://en.wikipedia.org/wiki
    /Baba_Yaga.

WORKS CITED

Balsam, Joel. "The Rougarou, Beast of the Louisiana Bayou, Gets a Makeover." *Atlas Obscura.* October 19, 2022. https://www.atlasobscura.com/articles/rougarou-louisiana.

Carboni, Stefano. "The 'Book of Surprises' (Kitab al-bulhan) of the Bodleian Library." *The La Trobe Journal.* Accessed September 1, 2023. https://www.slv.vic.gov.au/sites/default/files/La-Trobe-Journal-91-Stefano-Carboni.pdf.

"Chickcharney." *DBpedia.* Accessed September 1, 2023. https://dbpedia.org/page/Chickcharney.

"Chickcharney, Caribbean Folklore." *Northend Agent's* (blog). October 12, 2021. https://www.northendagents.com/chickcharney-caribbean-folklore/.

Cox, William T. *Fearsome Creatures of the Lumberwoods.* Washington, DC: Press of Judd & Detweiler, 1910.

WORKS CITED

Cursons, Meaghan. "Witches of the Woods." *The Collective Magazines.* Accessed August 2023. https://thecollectivemags.ca /witches-of-the-woods/.

Editors of Encyclopaedia Britannica. "Baba Yaga." *Britannica.* Updated November 29, 2023. https://www.britannica.com/topic /Baba-Yaga.

————. "Paul Bunyan." *Britannica.* Updated September 15, 2023. https://www.britannica .com/topic/Paul-Bunyan.

————. "Tree of Life." *Britannica.* Updated November 17, 2023. https://www.britannica .com/topic/tree-of-life-religion.

"Faun." *Wikipedia.* Last modified November 15, 2023. https://en.wikipedia.org/wiki/Faun.

"Fearsome critters." *Wikipedia.* Last modified September 28, 2023. https://en.wikipedia .org/wiki/Fearsome_critters.

WORKS CITED

Foltz, Chelsea. "A Brief History of Leprechauns,
    Ireland's Trickster Fairies." *The Real World.*
    March 9, 2020. https://www.trafalgar
    .com/real-word/history-of-leprechauns
    -trickster-fairies.

"Fox spirit." *Wikipedia.* Last modified November 16,
    2023. https://en.wikipedia.org/wiki
    /Fox_spirit.

"Hulder." *Wikipedia.* Last modified November 25,
    2023. https://en.wikipedia.org/wiki/Hulder.

"Huldra: The Alluring Forest Spirits of
    Scandinavian Folklore." *Surflegacy* (blog).
    Accessed August 1, 2023. https://surflegacy
    .net/huldra/.

"Huldra: The Norse Troll." *Mythlok* (blog).
    Accessed August 1, 2023. https://mythlok
    .com/huldra/.

WORKS CITED

"Huli Jing." *Academic Dictionaries and Encyclopedias.*
     Accessed September 1, 2023. https://
     vampire_mythology.en-academic
     .com/307/Huli_Jing.

"The Huli Jing [Chinese Mythology]."
     Bestiarium. Accessed September 1,
     2023. https://www.tumblr.com/
     bestiarium/682964440468127744/
     the-huli-jing-chinese-mythology-this-is.

"Information About Local Folk Characters."
     Internet Archive Wayback Machine. Updated
     October 29, 2002. https://web.archive.org
     /web/20101122082307/http://www.nalis
     .gov.tt/Folklore/folkcharacters.htm.

Kerner, Frank. "History of the Rougarou:
     Louisiana's Werewolf." *Pelican State of Mind*
     (blog). Accessed September 1, 2023. https://
     pelicanstateofmind.com/louisiana-love
     /history-rougarou-louisiana-werewolf/.

WORKS CITED

"Kitsune." *Wikipedia.* Last modified November 29, 2023. https://en.wikipedia.org/wiki/Kitsune.

"Kitsune." *Yokai.com* (blog). Accessed August 2023. https://yokai.com/kitsune/.

Koto, Koray. "The Tree of Life in Turkic Mythology." *Ulukayin.* March 10, 2021. https://ulukayin.org/the-tree-of-life-in -turkic-communities-with-its-current-effects/.

"Kumiho." *Wikipedia.* Last modified November 13, 2023. https://en.wikipedia.org/wiki /Kumiho.

Liles, Maryn. "30 Most Mythical Creatures from Folklore, Legends and Fairytales." *Parade.* September 29, 2022. https:// parade.com/1056247/marynliles /mythical-creatures/.

"Loup-Garous and Rougarous." *Maverick Werewolf* (blog). Accessed September 1, 2023. https:// maverickwerewolf.com/werewolf-facts /loup-garous-and-rougarous/.

WORKS CITED

Maines, James. "The Gumiho: Korea's Nine
      Tailed Fox." *KoreabyMe* (blog). Accessed
      September 1, 2023 https://koreabyme.com
      /the-gumiho-koreas-nine-tailed-fox/.

Mayntz, Melissa. "Cardinals: Legends, Lore,
      and Spiritual Symbolism." *Farmer's
      Almanac.* Updated May 2, 2022.
      https://www.farmersalmanac.com
      /cardinals-legends-lore-and-spiritual-symbolism.

McElhinney, David. "6 Things to Know About the
      Inari Fox in Japanese Folklore." *Japan Objects.*
      February 5, 2022. https://japanobjects.com
      /features/kitsune.

"Monster of the Week: Huli Jing." *The Supernatural
      Fox Sisters* (blog). August 9, 2016. https://
      thesupernaturalfoxsisters.com/2016/08/09
      /monster-of-the-week-huli-jing/.

"Monster of the Week: Kumiho." *The Supernatural
      Fox Sisters* (blog). June 3, 2015. https://

WORKS CITED

thesupernaturalfoxsisters.com/2015/06/03
/monster-of-the-week-kumiho/.

"Papa Bois." *Caribbean Reads* (blog). Accessed
September 1, 2023. https://www
.caribbeanreads.com/papa-bois/.

"Papa Bois." *Wikipedia.* Last modified September 5,
2023. https://en.wikipedia.org/wiki
/Papa_Bois.

"'Paul Bunyan,' an American Folk Tale." *VOA
Learning English.* May 5, 2023. https://
learningenglish.voanews.com/a/paul-bunyan
-american-folk-tale/4307240.html.

Renfro, Alisha. "Save the Swamp: But,
Beware the 'Rougarou.'" *National Wildlife
Federation* (blog). October 29, 2019.
https://blog.nwf.org/2019/10
/save-the-swamp-but-beware-the-rougarou/.

Schmitz, Nancy and Clayton Ma. "Loup-Garou."
The Canadian Encyclopedia. Updated August 20,

WORKS CITED

2021. https://www.thecanadianencyclopedia.
ca/en/article/loup-garou.

"The Legend of the Chickcharnies." *Exuma Online*
(blog). September 30, 2021. http://exuma
.online/culture/the-legend-of-chickcharnies/.

"The Traditional Japanese Kitsune Mask."
Eiyo Kimono (blog). August 30, 2022.
https://eiyokimono.com/a/blog
/japanese-kitsune-mask.

"Tree Concept in Turkish Culture." *Nanyang
Technological University* (blog). Accessed
September 1, 2023. https://blogs.ntu.edu.sg
/hp3203-2018-03/tree-of-life.

Tryon, Henry H. *Fearsome Critters.* Cornwall, NY:
The Idlewild Press, 1939.

"Ulukayin." *Wikipedia.* Last modified October
11, 2023. https://en.wikipedia.org/wiki
/Ulukay%C4%B1n.

WORKS CITED

"Waqwaq Tree." *Fandom.* Accessed September 1, 2023. https://mythus.fandom.com/wiki /Waqwaq_Tree.

Weiser, Kathy. "Paul Bunyan—Hero Lumberjack." *Legends of America* (blog). Updated May 2017. https://www.legendsofamerica.com /ah-paulbunyan/.

Zhelyazkov, Yordan. "Huldra: Seductive Forest Beings of Norse Mythology." *Symbolsage* (blog). August 6, 2023. https://symbolsage.com /huldra-norse-mythology/.

Zhelyazkov, Yordan. "Huli Jing: The Chinese Original Nine-Tailed Fox." *Symbolsage* (blog). June 3, 2022. https://symbolsage.com /huli-jing-nine-tailed-fox/.

INDEX

INDEX

INDEX

INDEX

ABOUT THE AUTHOR

JASON LANCASTER is a lover of folklore and a teacher in Portland, Oregon. He enjoys exploring the enchanted forests of the Pacific Northwest.

ABOUT THE ILLUSTRATOR

KATE FORRESTER is a freelance illustrator from the south coast of England. She specializes in creating bespoke hand-lettering and intricate illustrations for book covers, packaging, and many other applications. More than anything, Kate loves telling stories and collaborating with her clients and authors to bring their words to life.